NOTE TO

Apologetics Press is a non-profit organization dedicated to the defense of New Testament Christianity. For over a quarter of a century, we have provided faith-building materials for adults. We also have produced numerous materials (like *Discovery* magazine, our *Explorer Series*, and various books) for young people in third grade through high school. We now are pleased to present a new series of books for even younger children.

The Apologetics Press Early Reader Series is a set of books aimed at children in kindergarten through second grade. Depending on the age of your children, this series is flexible enough to allow parents to read to their children, read along with their children, or they can listen while their children read aloud to them.

The books in this series are filled with beautiful full-color pictures and wonderful information about God, His creation, and His Word. These books are written on a level that early readers will enjoy, while drawing them closer to their Creator.

We hope you enjoy using the Apologetics Press Early Reader Series to encourage your children to read, while at the same time helping them learn about God and His creation.

God Made the World

by Kyle Butt

Copyright © 2005
Apologetics Press

ISBN-10: 0-932859-69-0

ISBN-13: 978-0-932859-69-3

Library of Congress: 2005926995

Printed in China

God Made The World

by
Kyle Butt

DAY ONE

On day one,
God created
the Earth.
It was covered
by water.
The Earth was
very dark.

DAY

God also created
light.

He
separated
the light
from the
darkness.

He
called
the light
Day.

And He called
the darkness Night.

NIGHT

DAY TWO

On day two, God created the sky and air.

Animals and people breathe air. Without the sky and air, animals and people could not live.

DAY THREE

God made dry land on day three.
On the dry land God put trees,
flowers, and plants.
He made many different
kinds of plants.

Some plants are small, and grow pretty flowers.

Look at this pretty tulip.

Other plants are big, and
grow fruit that is
good to eat.
Look at
all the
tasty fruit.

Can you name the fruits?

Animals and people like to eat fruit.

But on day three of Creation, there were no animals or people. God had not created them yet.

Can you name these fruits?

Star Fruit

Mango

Papaya

DAY FOUR

On day four,
God created
the Sun,
Moon,
and stars.

He put the Sun
in the sky to
rule the day.

He put the
Moon in the
sky to rule
the night.

God put the stars
in the sky to shine
at night.

The Moon controls the oceans' tides.

The Sun helps plants make food.

Stars can be used to guide ships.

The Sun, Moon, and stars help us count time.

The Earth goes around the Sun in one year.

A full Moon shines about once a month.

DAY FIVE

God created the animals
in the seas and oceans
on day five.

Fish were
created on
day five.

Some fish are small and pretty,
like these colorful clown fish.

Other fish are big and ugly, like this grouper

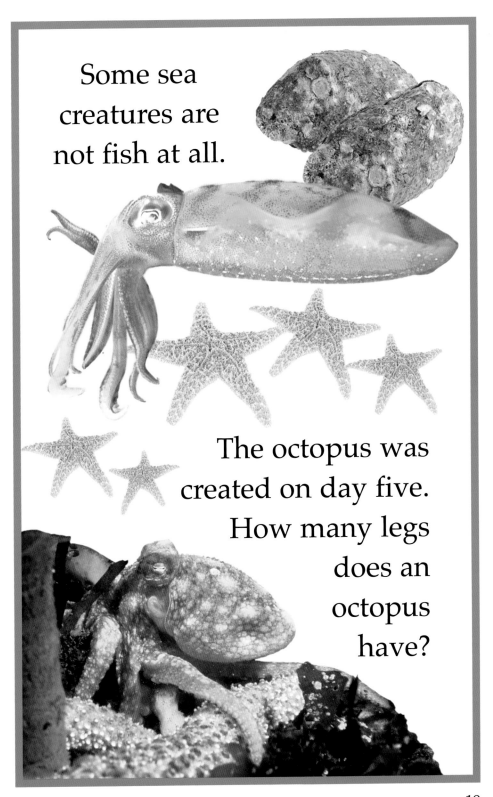

Some sea
creatures are
not fish at all.

The octopus was
created on day five.
How many legs
does an
octopus
have?

Sharks also
were created
on day five.
Some sharks are fast swimmers,
have many teeth,
and eat other
fish.

20

Whales are not fish, but they do live in the ocean. Some whales are the biggest animals alive.

These whales are as big as a large pick-up truck.

God also
created birds and
flying animals
on day five.

Birds come
in many
shapes and
sizes.

Some birds are small and pretty, like this humming bird.

Other birds are big and not very pretty, like this ground hornbill.

Birds like penguins swim in cold water.

Penguins cannot fly, but they can swim very fast.

They live where there is ice and snow.

Animals like bats can fly.

But bats are not birds.

They hang in dark caves. Some
bats fly at night and eat bugs.

DAY SIX

God made land animals on day six.

Look at the large elephant. It has a long trunk that it uses to get food. It also has long tusks.

Some land animals are very big.

Other animals are very little.

See the tiny mice.

Some animals live in trees.

Look at the monkey in the tree. Sometimes monkeys use their tails to hang on branches.

Other animals live in holes in the ground.

Prairie dogs dig tunnels under the ground.

God also made humans on day six.
Adam and Eve were the first two
humans. God made Adam first.

DAY SEVEN
God stopped creating on day seven.
When God was finished, He said
everything was very good.